...Greg Mey
tell you wha
be sure that you have it. This may be the most important book you will ever read. Perhaps, like me, you will look back decades from now and recall a book that you read that pointed you to Jesus and the certainty of personal salvation. This book can do just that. That is my prayer for you.

Derek W. H. Thomas
Senior Minister, First Presbyterian Church, Columbia, SC
Chancellor's Professor, Reformed Theological Seminary
Teaching Fellow, Ligonier Ministries

Justification has rightly been called the doctrine by which the church stands or falls. We may be thankful to Greg Meyer for an engaging and accessible introduction to this important biblical teaching. His concise chapters, engaging questions, and helpful glossary will serve beginning and seasoned readers alike. Read *Justification* and arise grateful to God for His amazing grace!

Guy Prentiss Waters
James M. Baird, Jr. Professor of New Testament,
Reformed Theological Seminary, Jackson, Mississippi

This short book is about being justified by faith. This is the central change in a person's relation to the Lord God his Creator. This is a change due to His pure grace, from death to life with God. Such a change enables a needy person to be a faithful follower of God's Son Jesus Christ. It brings him or her to have a trust in God, a heart of love for Him, and of hope to be in His eternal presence. So studying it and praying about it could turn the reader upside down.

Paul Helm
Emeritus Professor of the History and Philosophy of Religion, King's College, London

In a day-and-age where we set the bar way too low for our students by underestimating their cognitive abilities, we need to re-set the bar at the heights that foster deep spiritual growth – growth that will transform them both now and in the future. Greg Meyer has given us a tool we can use to instruct our students in one of the most foundational doctrines of the Christian faith. Use this book to launch your students into an awe-inspiring understanding of God's amazing grace.

Walt Mueller
President, Center for Parent/Youth Understanding

Greg Meyer has done a great service for the next generation of rising young people. Calvin said that justification by grace through faith was the hinge on which the church turned. Knowing that another generation can mine not only the theological significance, but the deeply pastoral encouragement of this great truth of the faith is enough to put a smile on the face of even the most cynical about tomorrow's church.

Les Newsom
Lead Pastor, Christ Presbyterian Church, Oxford, Mississippi

Greg Meyer is a wise, winsome, effective leader of youths and young adults. His knowledge of Scripture, joined with his knowledge of youth, make him the right person to teach young people the doctrine of justification and to explain why it matters.

Dan Doriani
Professor of Biblical Theology, Covenant Theological Seminary, St. Louis, Missouri

...In this short, accessible book, Meyer wrestles an enormously significant theological concept (as he puts it, 'lassoing the rhino') into language that his readers will be able to understand intellectually and emotionally, so that they can live out their justification practically. This book will help, comfort, and encourage the teens and youth pastors who read it; best of all, readers will love God more as they understand justification as the expression of God's unfailing love for us.

Anna Meade Harris
Editor-in-Chief, Rooted Ministry Blog

If a person can understand the doctrine of justification, then they can understand the core of the gospel and the Christian faith. It is the main highway through which all of Christianity flows. Greg Meyer has provided a clear, concise, and accessible even by which young Christians can grasp justification. This book will afford young readers better understanding of the glories and blessings of the gospel. I want my own children to read this book.

Cameron Cole
Founding Chairman, Rooted: Advancing Gospel-Centered Youth Ministry
Editor and author of several books

...If you do not adequately understand and believe that your forgiveness and acceptance by God is based on the righteousness of Christ alone, imputed to us, and received by faith alone, then your Christian experience is imperiled. But the sentence I have just said is a theological mouthful and needs unpacking in such a way that students and other Christians can accessibly understand it. Greg Meyer does that good work in this book, and I commend it to you for your growth in grace and sense of assurance of salvation.

Ligon Duncan
Chancellor and CEO, Reformed Theological Seminary

TRACK
DOCTRINE

GREG
MEYER

SERIES EDITED BY
JOHN PERRITT

A STUDENT'S GUIDE TO JUSTIFICATION

CHRISTIAN
FOCUS

tɥm

Copyright © Greg Meyer 2022

paperback ISBN 978-1-5271-0805-9
ebook ISBN 978-1-5271-0867-7

10 9 8 7 6 5 4 3 2 1

First published in 2022
by
Christian Focus Publications Ltd,
Geanies House, Fearn, Ross-shire,
IV20 1TW, Great Britain
www.christianfocus.com

with

Reformed Youth Ministries,
1445 Rio Road East
Suite 201D
Charlottesville,
Virginia, 22911

Cover by MOOSE77

Printed by Bell & Bain, Glasgow

CONTENTS

Series Introduction

Christianity is a religion of words, because our God is a God of words. He created through words, calls Himself the Living Word, and wrote a book (filled with words) to communicate to His children. In light of this, pastors and parents should take great efforts to train the next generation to be readers. *Track* is a series designed to do exactly that.

Written for students, the *Track* series addresses a host of topics in three primary areas: Doctrine, Culture, and the Christian Life. *Track's* booklets are theologically rich, yet accessible. They seek to engage and challenge the student without dumbing things down.

One definition of a track reads: *a way that has been formed by someone else's footsteps.* The goal of the *Track* series is to point us to that 'someone else' – Jesus Christ. The One who forged a track to guide His followers. While we cannot follow this track perfectly, by His grace and Spirit He calls us to strive to stay on the path. It is our prayer that this series of books would help guide Christ's Church until He returns.

In His service,

John Perritt
RYM's Director of Resources
Series Editor

Introduction: The A to Z

It has been a real joy of mine over the past few years to watch my oldest son learn to read and write. At first, he was mastering the alphabet – bit by bit. Next, he was identifying words through his newly acquired phonics skills. Then we were amazed to watch him begin reading short books. Before long, he was reading longer books – checking out piles of books each week from his school's library. Suddenly, it seemed, he was off and running into the reading world! Whole worlds of excitement, knowledge, wisdom, and possibilities opened up to him. However, though he had progressed to a more advanced level in his reading, he (and all of us too) always still required those basic, first bits of knowledge – mainly the alphabet. No matter how advanced we get in our learning, we can never leave the alphabet behind.

Similarly, in the Christian life, we need to remember our ABCs, if you will. The most foundational of the Christian ABCs is the gospel. Often, we can fall into thinking of the simple truths of the gospel story – Jesus' incarnation, life, teaching, death, resurrection, and ascension – as the elementary, first parts of Christian life that we 'understand' before moving on to more advanced stuff. While it's true that God desires us to grow more deeply into these truths, we never really leave them behind. Just like we never leave behind the alphabet, even if we're reading a textbook on quantum physics or ancient Greek philosophy.

Pastor Tim Keller captures this reality memorably for us when he writes:

> ...we never 'get beyond the gospel' to something more advanced. The gospel is not the first step in a stairway of truths; rather, it is more like the hub in a wheel of truth. The gospel is not just the ABCs but the A to Z of Christianity. The gospel is not the minimum required doctrine necessary to enter the kingdom but the way we make all progress in the kingdom. [1]

1   Keller, Timothy. 'The Centrality of the Gospel.' https://redeemercitytocity.com/articles-stories/the-

This is such an important truth to remember as you pick up a book like this on the doctrine of justification. No matter how old you are, how long you have gone to church, or how long you have followed Jesus, you still need to hear and be reminded of the good news of Christ – even when it is explained and summarized simply and concisely. It's the A to Z, not just the ABCs. The gospel always applies to you and your life at all times. It is the key that unlocks every door in the hallway of the Christian life. You're never too old, too smart, too accomplished, or too experienced to not need it.

So, the fact that you have picked up this book is a great thing! Because at the heart of the gospel of Jesus Christ is the doctrine of justification. It is a core truth and reality for every Christian. It is a great place to start if you are exploring Christianity and trying to make sense of what it is all about. Further, justification is fundamentally connected to other doctrines concerning salvation as well – such as adoption, sanctification, and glorification. Therefore, as we dig deeper into justification, we will find incredible life-giving truth, understand the

centrality-of-the-gospel

Bible better, meet with God Himself, and grow to become more mature believers.

Also, by deepening your understanding of what justification is and what it means for your life, you will find lasting comfort and joy. How is this? In justification we see the very heart of God displayed: His steadfast love for sinners, His free mercy and grace, and His perfect justice. So, whether you would call yourself a Christian or not, it is my hope for you as you read this book that you would experientially know Jesus and His grace more truly and deeply and in that 'find rest for your souls' (Matt. 11:29).

So, what is justification? Why is it important? To find out, I invite you to keep reading! Admittedly, justification is a churchy word that may be new to you. There will be other words and phrases like it along the way as well (perhaps you've already read a few churchy words in this short intro?). Because of this, there is a short glossary at the back of the book for you to use as you read. Use it when you encounter a word or phrase that is unfamiliar or confusing.

1. Why is Justification Important?

============

THE IMPORTANCE OF ASKING WHY

'Why?' This is the question my children ask me the most. 'Why do I have to get ready for school? Why do I have to do my homework right now? Why can't we have something else for dinner?' While I have to confess that I do get annoyed by these questions at times, 'why questions' are incredibly important when it comes to our motivation and understanding as we learn and grow. Often if we know why something is important, we have an easier time jumping into it, sustaining our focus, and have the motivation to think, learn, and respond.

This is an especially important question to ask of the teachings of the Bible, the Holy Scriptures. We may want to rush into the 'what questions,' but answering the 'why questions' is where we will find the needed drive to properly engage with the answers to the 'what questions.' Without the clarifying energy and curiosity of the 'why questions' we may not be able to sustain our investigation of the topic.

So, in an effort to apply this to our present topic: *Why is justification important? Why read a book about justification?* Let me give you a few answers to that.

OUR PROBLEM: THE 'BAD NEWS' OF THE GOSPEL

In the movie *Apollo 13,* the American astronauts on their mission to the moon realize that their spacecraft has sustained critical damage during one of their operational procedures. Strange things are happening to the crew as they struggle to make sense of what has happened to them. Eventually, Captain Jim Lovell, after analyzing the catastrophic results, says to mission control, 'Houston, we have a problem.' Their mission and their very lives were in peril and they now knew it.

Similar to Lovell and his crew, we have a problem! A big problem. A life-or-death size problem. While the Bible is about the 'good news' of Jesus Christ at its core, this wonderful news is preceded by inescapable 'bad news.' In fact, the 'good news' of Christ is the answer and response to this 'bad news.'

So, what is this bad news?

The Apostle Paul sums it up well in Romans 3:22b-23 where he writes, 'For there is no distinction: for all have sinned and fall short of the glory of God.' The bad news is that we have sinned against our Creator, the holy and just God, and, as a result, we are alienated from Him, others, and even ourselves. As Paul goes on to say in Ephesians 2:1-3, we are all spiritually 'dead in our trespasses and sins,' 'sons [and daughters] of disobedience,' and 'by nature children of wrath.' Not only has our sin separated us from God, but we are unable to close the gap or remedy the situation. We cannot save ourselves! Spiritually, we're dead, prone to wander in selfish disobedience, and rightfully deserve and experience the anger of God. We justly deserve God's punishment and the eternal torment of hell.

This is bad news! But we need to hear it, understand it, and embrace it in order for the good news to be truly good to us. Without believing the bad news, the good news will not be good to us and Jesus will be meaningless. We will remain separated from God, ourselves, and others. J.C. Ryle said it well when he wrote, 'The plain truth is that a right knowledge of

sin lies at the root of all saving Christianity.'[1]
We must acknowledge and confess our sin –
our willful rebellion and spiritual inability –
in order to make any headway. Salvation is
available to us, but it depends on believing the
bad news about ourselves first. This is a life-or-
death problem.

THE CORE OF THE GOOD NEWS

This is where justification comes in. The
doctrine of justification is the good news
answer to our pressing life-or-death problem
of sin and death. J.I. Packer suggests that this
Christian teaching is 'the heart of gospel' as
far as the Apostle Paul is concerned.[2] Sinclair
Ferguson, echoing the Protestant Reformer,
Martin Luther, indicates that justification is not
only 'the article by which the church stands
or falls...but also of the standing or falling of
Christianity.'[3] Justification is at the very core of
the good news of the gospel of Jesus Christ and
is the source of life for the Church of Christ.

1   Ryle, J.C. *Holiness* (Grand Rapids: Baker, 1979), 1-2.

2   Packer, J.I. *Concise Theology: A Guide to Historic
    Christian Beliefs* (Downers Grove, IL: IVP, 1993), 164.

3   Ferguson, Sinclair B. *The Christian Life: A Doctrinal
    Introduction* (Edinburgh: Banner of Truth, 1981), 80.

This is why the doctrine of justification is important: it's a fundamental doctrine of the Christian faith that speaks to our greatest human need – the forgiveness of our sins, becoming holy in God's sight, and the reconciliation of all relationships. The most important relationship being that with our Creator. If you can understand and embrace this doctrine, you will have a firm foundation to stand on and a path toward peace and joy in fellowship with God through an abiding relationship with Jesus Christ.

Main Point

Justification is important because it is at the heart of the good news response to the bad news of our sinfulness.

Questions for Reflection

- How does the 'bad news' we find in the Bible prepare us to receive and embrace its 'good news' ?
- What does 'a right knowledge of sin' look like?
- What kinds of forgiveness and reconciliation do you hope and long for in your life?

2. What is Justification?

LASSOING A RHINO

Animals in the wild are breathtaking. We forget this as we go about our typically tame lives in the more developed parts of the world. But the peculiarity, ferocity, and reckless abandon with which they live still fill us with wonder. This is why there are so many animal adventure TV shows and movies! We love watching people more daring than us get close to these incredible creatures to study, document, and share their wild ways.

So, why am I talking about wild animals in a book on the doctrine of justification? Well, trying to summarize and define a theological teaching as important and expansive as justification can feel like trying to lasso a wild rhinoceros. It can feel like an impossibly daunting task to mine the Bible and bring clarity to such a wildly powerful aspect of

God's salvation of His people. Thankfully, we are not the first to do so. The 'rhinoceros' of justification will never be tamed, but there is much we know from the Scriptures themselves as well as theologians of the past who have brought clarity to this teaching through their own scholarship.

GETTING SOME DEFINITION

One group of people we can benefit from in our study of justification are the Westminster Divines – a group of seventeenth-century English and Scottish pastors and theologians. This might sound boring to some of you, but hear me out because their work is still helpful for us today. In their years of deliberation and study, they produced the Westminster Confession of Faith and Catechisms. Their Westminster Shorter Catechism gives us the most concise definition:

Justification is an act of God's free grace, wherein He pardons all our sins, and accepts us as righteous in His sight, only for the righteousness of Christ imputed to us, and received by faith alone.[1]

---

1   Westminster Shorter Catechism, Q&A #33.

I understand the above definition contains those 'churchy words' we talked about earlier, but we'll unpack this in just a bit.

What the Westminster Divines are getting at here is that in justification God declares us to be forgiven and holy in His sight because He has established a new relationship with us. He did this through the life, death, and resurrection of His Son, Jesus Christ. Jesus lived the righteous life we failed to live, died the death we deserved to die, and triumphed over death so that we might be brought into the family of God and obtain eternal life. All that Christ earned we receive through faith in Him alone, which is a gift of God's grace.[2] In justification, God's love overflows in grace to spiritually dead sinners whom He has called to Himself to be His children. The unlovely and loveless are accounted lovely because of the love of Christ. The unrighteous become righteous through the obedience, sacrifice, and new life of the Righteous One. In answer to our 'bad news,' justification is truly 'good news.'

---

2   Murray, John. *Redemption Accomplished and Applied* (Grand Rapids, MI: Eerdmans, 2015), 123-25.

WHAT JUSTIFICATION IS AND IS NOT

Though the rest of this book will further unpack justification as a doctrine, there are a few broader aspects of it that we can clarify at this point. First of all, justification is an 'act of God.' It is something God does without our help. Further, it is a 'judicial' act. God, as the Righteous Judge, is declaring something about us as if in a courtroom setting. In justification, instead of receiving the 'guilty' verdict we justly deserve, God declares us to be innocent in His sight on account of Christ's righteousness being applied to us. When God looks at us now, He sees Jesus.

Secondly, in justification, God remedies our twofold problem: our sin before God and our lack of necessary righteousness. Through the work of Jesus Christ, God addresses both. Jesus stood in our place as the sacrifice for our sin in His death on the Cross. But, in addition to this, Jesus also lived a life of perfect holiness that was always pleasing to the Father in our place (John 8:29). Our sins are placed on Christ while His righteousness is 'imputed' or attributed to us – as if it were ours. So not only do we not get the punishment we deserve, we also get riches that we don't deserve! The Apostle Paul sums up this 'Great Exchange' well in 2 Corinthians 5:21 when he writes, 'For our sake [God] made [Jesus] to be sin who knew no sin, so that in him we might become the righteousness of God.' Incredibly, through Jesus' death on the Cross, God maintains His justice while also being 'the justifier of the one who has faith in Jesus' (Rom. 3:26).

Finally, in justification, these benefits of forgiveness and righteousness are only received by faith in Christ, which is itself a gift of God's grace (Eph. 2:8-9). We do not 'do' anything to be justified. Our good works do not earn us a justified status (Gal. 2:16; Phil. 3:9). We simply receive and rest in what Christ has already accomplished for us by faith. In this, justification reverses our natural approach to God. It humbles us and ought to stop any boasting on our part (Rom. 3:27).

A few years ago, my wife and I were in Chicago for conference with another couple. Before the trip, the husband suggested we go to eat at a particular restaurant because his cousin was CEO of the chain to which it belonged. What we didn't realize until later was that this restaurant was on the 65th floor of the Willis Tower (one of the tallest buildings in the world). When we arrived, we proceeded to the security desk and were told that our friends were already waiting for us. Quickly, we began to realize we were in for a treat when the security guard gave us special badges, directed us to another security area, and a VIP elevator.

Up we went, getting excited as each floor zoomed by us. Upon reaching the restaurant we were personally greeted by the staff and escorted to a private dining area where we met our friends. As we sat down and settled in, we marveled at the place. It got even better when our friends explained that the whole 5-star meal was on-the-house – all because of my friend's cousin! We gave the staff his name and we were accepted as if we were him. We were welcomed in for a beautiful night of good food, friendship, and rejoicing.

This is what justification is like. Even though we don't belong, we are accepted as if we are a VIP – all because of the name and work of another. Simply by receiving this grace, we enjoy access to a feast of blessing, forever accounted as worthy and acceptable – forever loved. The gospel of Christ is so good!

Main Point

By faith alone, Justification grants forgiveness to sinners and declares them righteous because of Jesus' righteous life, death, and resurrection.

Questions for Reflection

- Drawing from Westminster's definition of justification, how would you define it in your own words?
- What tends to trouble you more personally: your sinfulness (the bad things you've done) or your lack of righteousness (the goodness you lack)? Why is a consideration of both of these things essential for a deeper embrace of the gospel?
- Have you ever had an experience like being a VIP somewhere? What would it mean for you if you experienced this with God?

3. The Story of Justification, Part 1

BEHIND THE MUSIC

Music is a big part of my life. Some of this is because I am a musician, but more of it has to do with my love of stories. The stories and poetry of the songs draw me in, but so do the stories of the artists who make the music. I often read the Wikipedia and fan pages of bands that I like. I watch band interviews, portions of live shows, and music commentary on YouTube. Like the old VH1 TV show from the 1990s and 2000s, I want to know the story 'behind the music.'

Just as there is passion, feeling, and a story of relationship behind the music of our favorite bands, there is a story behind the music of God's grace to us in justification. His love and faithfulness fuel all that He has done and will do for His people. The doctrine of justification is not just something that we find taught in the New Testament. It has its roots in the story of salvation that started at the very beginning. There is a story side to justification, and it has to do with the Old Testament idea of 'covenant' and what theologians call 'Covenant Theology.'

WHAT IN THE WORLD IS A COVENANT?

It can be difficult to read the Bible, right? Making sense of where each book fits into the whole and how to read each portion can be challenging. Even though this can be a struggle, Covenant Theology is something that can actually help us understand the story of the Bible better. Covenant Theology is the way that the Bible actually structures itself as a story of God's redemption of His people. It gives us a framework for understanding the story of the Bible, while also assuring us of God's great love for us.

So, what is a covenant? Buckle up for some churchy words. A covenant is an expression of God 'coming down to our level' to help us in our state as needy sinners, by binding Himself to us in love through the making of promises.[1] A covenant is 'a bond in blood sovereignly administered.'[2] It is a relationship of love that

---

1   Westminster Confession of Faith, 7.1.

2   Robertson, O. Palmer, *The Christ of the Covenants* (Phillipsburg, NJ: P&R, 1981), 4.

leads to a contract being made between the two parties. Life-and-death promises (or vows) are made from one to the other. Blessings and curses are associated with keeping and breaking these agreements.

A modern example of this is what we see in the 'covenant of marriage.' A husband and wife, who love each other, bind themselves together legally by the making of promises and vows before witnesses. Tokens of their love and promises are given in the form of rings that are exchanged. Ultimately, the married couple's love and commitment to one another is signified and sealed by the consummation of a sexual relationship and a life together. Through this their love and commitment have the opportunity to flow out in blessing through their children and their life in the broader community.

In the Bible, the idea of covenant becomes visible at the beginning of humanity's relationship with God. Out of love, the Triune God – Father, Son, and Holy Spirit – creates mankind and makes promises to Adam and Eve. God's covenant love is the foundation and driver of the whole story of Scripture.

THE COVENANT OF CREATION

The first place in the Bible that we see God making a covenant with His people is with Adam in the Garden of Eden. It is called the Covenant of Creation or also the Covenant of Works. In Genesis 1–2, we see God's great love for Adam and Eve as Creator and Father cause Him to bless them (Gen. 1:28-30; 2:9) and make promises to them. The main promise that He makes to them concerns two trees in the Garden. The 'tree of life' was a sign to them of the blessing of eternal life that would be theirs as a result of faithful obedience. Concerning the other tree, 'the tree of the knowledge of good and evil,' Adam and Eve were given a prohibition:

You may surely eat of every tree of the garden, but of the tree of the knowledge of good and evil you shall not eat, for in the day that you eat of it you shall surely die. (Gen. 2:16-17)

Unfortunately, when tempted by the serpent, Adam and Eve disobey God and break His covenant with them (Gen. 3:1-13). As a result of their sin, they are alienated from God and each other, experience pain and shame, and will now experience death (Gen. 3:14-24). This is the origin of the 'bad news' we previously discussed.

THE COVENANT OF GRACE

As you already know, this is not where the story ends. There is good news! Adam and Eve deserve instant death, but God has mercy on them. God makes another covenant with them now that the first has been broken. This covenant is called the Covenant of Grace. We see the seeds of this covenant embedded in the middle of God's cursing of the serpent:

> *I will put enmity between you and the woman, and between your offspring and her offspring; he shall bruise your head, and you shall bruise his heel. (Gen. 3:15)*

God declares that the serpent's (Satan) days are numbered. A male descendent of Eve will strike the death blow to him and an extended battle, though this descendent will be wounded in the process. This is a huge promise! He even pictures this coming sacrifice by killing animals to provide coverings for Adam and Eve in their nakedness and shame (Gen. 3:21).

As you may have guessed, the Sunday School answer of 'Jesus' applies to who this descendent ends up being. However, without jumping too far ahead yet, we can appreciate that this promise is the basis for the Covenant of Grace that will continue to unfold and intensify as the story of the Bible continues. God continues to act in faithful, gracious love by making a covenant to preserve the earth and mankind after Noah and the flood (Gen. 9). Yet, it is not until the Covenant of Grace is unfolded further in God's covenant with Abraham (Gen. 12–21) that we see more clearly how justification is fundamental to our relationship with God.

Main Point

Justification is part of the grand story of God's love and salvation that is unfolded in the Bible.

Questions for Reflection

- How well do you understand the big story of the Bible? How could you grow in your understanding of its story?
- How does the idea of covenant help us make sense of how God relates to humanity? What does it reveal about God?
- How are the Covenant of Creation and Covenant of Grace similar? How are they different?

4. The Story of Justification, Part 2

NOT SURE HOW I GOT HERE

A few years ago, I read an article entitled, 'The Anatomy of an NBA Entourage.'[1] In it, the author described the different types of people that you find included in the inner circle of professional basketball players like superstars LeBron James, Kevin Durant, and Steph Curry. There are close friends and family, business guys, random service guys (like barbers and DJs), bodyguards, and distant family and friends. However, my favorite is the last category of people you find in the posse: the 'Not Sure How I Got Here, but I'm Going to Milk It for All It's Worth' guys. They don't belong, but somehow these people have gotten close to someone great. As a result, they get to enjoy

---

1   Petkac, Luke. Bleacher Report article. https://bleacherreport.com/articles/1558549-the-anatomy-of-an-nba-entourage

many of the benefits associated with being a professional athlete – access to exclusive places as well as the enjoyment of expensive and exciting experiences.

This is the story of God's people. It's our story. It's the story of justification. Though we don't belong, because we're associated by faith to Someone great we get all sorts of benefits! It's an incredible thing to be a 'Not Sure How I Got Here' person. All Christians have an experience of this grace. So did Abraham.

ABRAHAM COUNTED AS RIGHTEOUS

As the story of the Bible continues on past Adam, Eve, and Noah, God unfolds the Covenant of Grace further. The biggest leap forward in terms of the clarity and intimacy of the covenant is in the story of Abraham, who was originally named Abram. Abraham was a nobody from nowhere. He grew up in a family that worshiped false gods (Josh. 24:2). And yet, God called Abraham to leave his home and follow Him (Gen. 12:1-3). God was determined to bless him – making Abraham's name great, making him a great nation, and giving him and his descendants land in which to live. All of this was undeserved. Abraham was not righteous. It was all of grace.

Incredibly, even though Abraham has several detours in his journey and missteps along the way (Gen. 13; 16), he responds to God's gracious promises with faith and trust. This continued to be the pattern in the four scenes where God unfolds and reaffirms His covenant with Abraham and his family (Gen. 12; 15; 17; 21). Even when Abraham doubts God's promises (Gen. 15:2-3), God continues to assure Abraham of His love. In response, Abraham takes God at His Word and has faith in God's promises. This is where we see the doctrine of justification on display. We are told that Abraham 'believed the Lord, and [God] counted it to him as righteousness' (Gen. 15:6). Abraham, who was a sinner like us, believed God's great, covenant promises and God credited that faith as righteousness. Because of his faith in God's promises, Abraham was counted as holy in God's sight – forgiven, beloved, and whole. By grace through faith he was saved.

The Apostle Paul picks up on this in the book of Romans. He indicates that the incredible experience of justification is available to all who trust in God's promises like Abraham:

But the words 'it was counted to him' were not written for his sake alone, but for ours also. It will be counted to us who believe in him who raised from the dead Jesus our Lord, who was delivered up for our trespasses and raised for our justification. (Rom. 4:23-25)

Just as Abraham looked forward to the promises of God that would ultimately be fulfilled in Jesus, we look back and trust in what Christ has already accomplished. Though there is more definition and clarity for us now as New Testament believers, justification has been at the heart of God's story of salvation from the very beginning. We are all 'Not Sure How I Got Here' people.

THE REST OF THE STORY

The amazing story of justification continues throughout the Old and New Testaments as God unfolds the mystery of the Covenant of Grace. While God binds Himself in covenant to a person and a family in Abraham, He binds Himself to the whole nation of Israel through their experience of the Exodus from Egypt and the giving of the Law at Mount Sinai. This is often called the Mosaic Covenant, where Moses acted as the people's covenant representative before God.

In fact, the tablets of the Ten Commandments are actually covenant documents – a collection of laws with associated blessings and curses with the grace of God's salvation in the Exodus serving as the basis for the relationship (Exod. 20:2).

The story moves forward further in God's covenant with David as he becomes King of Israel. At this point, God binds Himself in covenant with His people by establishing an everlasting kingdom through the line of David. In 2 Samuel 7, when David expresses his intention to build God a house in the temple, God counters by expressing His desire to build David's 'house' – a dynasty of kings culminating in Jesus, the Son of God and Son of David. Again, like Abraham and the nation of Israel, David did not deserve this blessing! He was an adulterer and murderer (2 Sam. 11–12) as well as an absent father. Even so, David believed God's promises and responded in faith. This is the story of justification.

And yet, this is not the end of the story as the Covenant of Grace eventually culminates in the New Covenant. This New Covenant is foretold in the prophets (Jer. 31:31-34) and pictured in the Old Testament administration of the Covenant of Grace, but comes to fruition in the birth, life, death, and resurrection of Jesus (Luke 22:20). We will unpack some of this in more detail in later chapters.

THE STORY CONTINUES

Though the story of justification begins in the Bible, it continues in more recent history and in our lives today. Since it is a teaching that is at the core of the gospel, it has been a doctrine that has had to be clarified, expounded, and defended through the history of the Church. Though there were debates about justification in the Early Church, this process came to a head in the Protestant Reformation during the sixteenth century in Europe. J.I. Packer asserts that justification was 'the storm center of the Reformation' as Martin Luther in Germany, John Calvin in France and Switzerland, and many others worked to bring clarity to Scripture's teaching in contrast to the Roman Catholic Church's deviation from the truth.[2]

Since that time and in every generation, the story of justification continues as the doctrine

---

2   Packer, J.I. *Concise Theology*, 164.

has lasting importance and centrality for all who seek to know the true and living God. The purity of Bible teaching in this area is essential for the Church as it seeks to remain faithful and vibrant. Without justification at the center, the gospel ceases to be good news and we begin telling a different story. Whereas if we continue to trust in Jesus alone as our righteousness and salvation today, we participate in the grand story of justification and bear witness to the world about the faithful love of our covenant-making God.

Main Point

Justification is part of the grand story of God's covenant love on full display.

Questions for Reflection

- Have you ever experienced some kind of benefit simply by being close to or connected to someone else? If so, what was it like? What did you gain from that association?
- How is Abraham a 'Not Sure How I Got Here' person? How are all Christians 'Not Sure How I Got Here' people?

- Why is justification an essential part of the big story of the Bible and of the Church's history?

5. The Source and Grounds of Justification

THE MIGHTY MISSISSIPPI

Growing up in the South and living for a time in Mississippi, the Mississippi River has been a fixture in my imagination. I live in St. Louis, Missouri, now and our city is pressed up to the river. It is an amazing and breathtaking sight as the second longest river in North America. While I knew some facts and heard many stories about the river growing up, I never actually knew what the source of this great river was. Do you? The traditional source of the Mississippi River is Lake Itasca in northern Minnesota. Minnesota! I would have never guessed it. This great, surging force flows from a mostly unknown and unrecognized source.

THE SOURCE OF JUSTIFICATION

In a similar way, the great doctrine of justification has an often-unrecognized source. What is it? Theologian Sinclair Ferguson writes, 'The love of God is the source of our justification.'[1] God's boundless *love* for His people is the source of justification. This great truth of God forgiving and making right His rebellious people flows from this key source.

Is this surprising or unexpected to you? Our arts and culture are saturated with stories about love. But what does God's love look like? Often the fact that God is our Creator and Judge can crowd out that He is also, and even more fundamentally, our loving Father. Michael Reeves points this out when he writes,

For if, before all things, God was eternally a Father, then this God is an inherently outgoing, life-giving God. He did not give life for the first time when he decided to create; from eternity he has been life-giving.[2]

God creates and gives life because He is our Father. Love flows out of Him naturally as it is fundamental to who He is. The Apostle John reminds us of this when he writes, 'God is love, and whoever abides in love abides in God, and

---

1 Ferguson, Sinclair B. *The Christian Life*, 85.

2 Reeves, Michael. *Delighting in the Trinity: An Introduction to the Christian Faith* (London: IVP Academic, 2012), 24.

God abides in him' (1 John 4:16). Even further, as Reeves touches on, God as a Triune (three-in-one) God has always been life-giving. He is love and has always been expressing that love in the community of Himself – between the Father, Son, and Holy Spirit eternally.

So how does this love spill out in the great river of justification? The Apostle John clarifies this as well when he writes,

> *In this the love of God was made manifest among us, that God sent his only Son into the world, so that we might live through him. In this is love, not that we have loved God but that he loved us and sent his Son to be the propitiation for our sins. (1 John 4:9-10)*

The next time you're bored in a sermon, or struggling to connect in a Bible study, remind yourself that you are part of the biggest romance of all time. The reason these theological truths are important to grasp is that they are wonderful, comforting, life-changing truths! The love of God for us is expressed most gloriously in our justification. The Father's love led Him to send the Son. The Son's love led Him to come, to live, to die, and to rise again. The Spirit's love leads Him to cultivate faith in us, apply this great salvation to us, and to assure us of God's great love for us. God's love is the source of the great river of forgiveness, justification, and propitiation (the absorbing of God's wrath against us). There's a reason one of the best-known Bible verses begins: 'For God so loved the world…' (John 3:16). This love is costly, unchanging, and completely selfless.

THE GROUNDS OF JUSTIFICATION

The love of God is the source of our justification, but as Ferguson goes on to say, 'the death of Christ is its grounds.'[3] While justification flows from God's love, it begins in the death of Christ as the culmination of His total obedience. Like a well-built building with a solid concrete foundation, our justification rests upon the finished work of Christ. Ferguson summarizes this well when he writes,

We 'have now been justified by [Jesus'] blood' (Rom. 5:9); the result of his obedient life and death is our justification (Rom. 5:18); just as he was delivered over to death for our sins he was raised because of our justification (Rom. 4:25).[4]

---

3   Ferguson, Sinclair B. *The Christian Life*, 85.

4   Ibid.

The grounds (or basis) of our justification is not our own goodness. It's not because of our good deeds. It's not even because of our faith in Jesus. Jesus' work on our behalf is the only grounds for our justification. In fact, this is the very point that the Apostle Paul works hard to make in Romans 1:18–3:20. Though no one is righteous and can approach God, Christ the Righteous One sacrifices Himself as a payment for our sin and gives us His perfect righteousness as a free gift of grace received by faith alone (2 Cor. 5:21).

ACTIVE AND PASSIVE

Theologians have often broken down the work of Christ into two categories: Christ's active obedience and His passive obedience. Christ's active obedience is the life He lived in total obedience to God. Jesus was born sinless as the incarnate Son of God and from birth until death lived a totally sinless and obedient life – in thought, word, and deed. He was 'born under the law' and lived a completely holy life – all for the sake of identifying with us and redeeming us from the curse of the law (Gal. 4:4; Heb 7:26; Gal. 3:10-14). Jesus actively obeyed His Father in everything, which ultimately culminated in His willing death on the Cross.

And this is what is meant by Christ's passive obedience: His sacrificial death for sinners. As the sinless One, He suffered and died for us guilty sinners that we might be declared innocent. As Derek Thomas is fond of saying: 'Christ received the covenant curse so that we might receive the covenant blessing.' In the Cross, He gets what we have earned (death) and gives us what He earned (eternal life). Incredibly, in this God remains just by punishing sin, while at the same time being 'the justifier of the one who has faith in Jesus' (Rom. 3:26).

This is the crucial and sometimes underemphasized aspect of justification: we receive Christ's righteousness! Christ's perfect, finished work is credited to our account! Yes, forgiveness is essential, but that only gets us half way there. What we also need is to be made perfectly righteous. Only then are we justified and made right before God. Just as a peanut butter and jelly sandwich is incomplete (and many would argue unsatisfying) without the jelly, without receiving Christ's righteousness by faith our salvation remains incomplete.

NO HOPE WITHOUT IT

In the end, the work of Christ on our behalf ought to be a precious and comforting truth to us. In all our discussion of being declared innocent or guilty, eternity is at stake. If you accept God's exchange, you can rest in His love because Christ has lived and died on your behalf. His resurrection guarantees and seals these benefits to you eternally. Pastor and theologian, J. Gresham Machen, on his deathbed dictated a last message to a dear friend that read: 'I'm so thankful for the active obedience of Christ: no hope without it.' These truths gave Machen great comfort even in that dark hour of death. They ought to give us that same unshakeable hope. Even in our darkest moments, we can rejoice along with the hymn:

Jesus, Thy blood and righteousness
My beauty are, my glorious dress;
Midst flaming worlds, in these arrayed,
With joy shall I lift up my head.[5]

---

5   Nicoalus Ludwig von Zinzendorf trans. by John Wesley, 'Jesus, Thy Blood and Righteousness.'

Main Point

Justification has its source in the love of God and has the work of Christ as its grounds.

Questions for Reflection

- Why might it be surprising that God's love is the source of justification?
- How is Jesus' death (and His total obedience leading up to that death) the grounds of justification?
- Why ought these truths naturally fill us with hope and confidence?
- In light of this teaching, how can we go about cultivating a deeper hope in Christ and His finished work?

6. The Instrument of Justification

One of the joys of parenting is getting to experience the things you loved as a child with your own kids. This occurred to me when I took two of my sons to an interactive children's museum a few years ago. At this amazing place, they had what is called a water table. It is a fun device where kids get to experiment with how water flows, while getting to play with toy boats and other items. Getting a little mischievous, we used the little walls you can put in place to keep all the water on one side of the table. One side was full and overflowing. The other was dry and lifeless. And there was no channel between them.

This is like our relationship with Jesus without faith. He is full of life, love, grace, and righteousness, while we are dead in our trespasses and sins, on our way to eternity without God. Our greatest need is forgiveness and righteousness, but we have no way of securing it by our own efforts.

This is where faith comes in. Faith, in the biblical sense, is the instrument of justification. It is the channel by which all of Christ's blessings and benefits become ours. Like parallel lines that never meet without a bridge, faith serves as the bridge and channel between Christ and us. Our faith, which is itself a gift of God's grace, is the means by which we receive God's forgiveness and Christ's righteousness. As Scripture says in many places, we are justified 'through faith' (Rom. 3:28; Gal. 2:16; Eph. 2:8). By faith, and by faith alone, are we justified.

WHAT IS 'SAVING' FAITH?

What faith is and how it works can be confusing. If you've ever been worried about whether you have 'enough' faith to be saved, you need to understand that while faith is something we do, it's not a 'work.' Moreover, there is a difference between general faith (believing God exists, etc.) and what theologians call 'saving' faith. J.C. Ryle provides some clarity to what is meant by saving faith when he writes:

True faith has nothing whatsoever of merit about it, and in the highest sense cannot be called 'a work.' It is by laying hold of a Saviour's hand, leaning on a husband's arm, and receiving a physician's medicine. It brings with it nothing to Christ but a sinful man's soul. It gives nothing, contributes nothing, pays nothing, performs nothing. It only receives, takes, accepts, grasps, and embraces the glorious gift of justification which Christ bestows, and by renewed daily acts enjoys that gift.[1]

Put even more succinctly, in true, saving faith we say to God: 'Nothing in my hand I bring, simply to Thy cross I cling.'[2] Similar to the water table my sons and I played with, faith becomes the channel of God's grace to us in the gospel. It is the instrument and means by which justification becomes really and truly ours. The Westminster Shorter Catechism defines it in the following way:

*Faith in Jesus Christ is a **saving grace**, whereby we **receive** and **rest** upon him alone for salvation, as he is offered to us in the gospel.*

---

1   Ryle, J.C. *Old Paths*, (Cambridge: James Clarke, 1977), 228.

2   Toplady, Augustus, 'Rock of Ages, Cleft for Me'.

Let's unpack this definition in a few chunks.

FAITH IS A SAVING GRACE

When the Catechism says that faith is a 'saving grace,' it means that faith is ultimately something that has its life in God – it is given by Him. Our faith develops and springs to life because God has worked in our hearts by the power of His Holy Spirit. This makes sense biblically because, as we have seen before, we are spiritually 'dead' in our sins unless Christ makes us alive (Eph. 2:1-3). Our true faith in Christ is only possible when God graciously enables us to trust in Him. In this, we can confess with the hymnwriter:

> *My Lord I did not choose you*
> *For that could never be*
> *My heart would still refuse you*
> *If you had not chosen me.*[3]

Faith is therefore a grace – a 'free gift,' just as Christ's work on our behalf is a freely given gift (Rom. 5:15). But, even more so, faith is a *saving* grace. Like a superhero movie, we have been snatched from certain death (and in our case, hell) and our ultimate 'happy ending' is

---

3   Conder, Josiah alt. Matthew S. Smith, 'My Lord I Did Not Choose You.'

that we will spend eternity with our Savior. But the gifts don't stop there. 'By' or 'through' faith we are justified; we receive all the good things promised to the children of God. This includes spiritual growth like our sanctification and glorification (Rom. 8:29-30) as well as the 'fruit of the Spirit' being evidenced in our lives (Gal. 5:22-23). Our salvation in Christ is a full salvation and it is all of grace through faith.

FAITH IS RECEIVING

While the Catechism describes the nature of faith, it also instructs us on what faith does or how faith works. First of all, faith involves 'receiving.' In saving faith, we 'receive... [Christ] alone for salvation, as he is offered to us in the gospel.' Faith is not a work, it's not something we can take pride in. It is simply the receiving of what Christ has accomplished. Instead of trying to prove ourselves or make ourselves acceptable to God, we receive what Christ has already done. We trust that He has provided and that it is enough – for our forgiveness and for our righteousness. This requires us to be humble and accept that we can't earn our own salvation. Like Ryle pointed out to us earlier, in true faith we are simply taking the medicine given by the Great Physician and leaning upon the arm of our Good Shepherd. As a beggar reaches out to receive food or money that is offered, in faith, we stretch out to receive spiritual food and wealth.[4] We believe and we are saved. In Christ, we are counted as righteous.

FAITH IS RESTING

In addition to receiving, faith also involves our *resting upon* Christ alone. Chad Van Dixhoorn reflects on this aspect of saving faith when he writes:

Faith is just resting on what Jesus has done. Faith is the abandoning of any attempt to please God on our own with our goodness, and trusting in Christ and his righteousness.[5]

Because we are justified by faith in what Christ has done, we can rest from all of our self-salvation projects. Naturally, we live with this overwhelming stress and pressure to prove ourselves. You may not realize it, but this is the

---

4   Waters, Guy, *A Christian's Pocket Guide to Being Made Right with God* (Fearn: Christian Focus Publications, 2012), 21.

5   Van Dixhoorn, Chad, *Confessing the Faith: A Reader's Guide to the Westminster Confession of Faith* (Edinburgh: Banner of Truth, 2014), 163.

default of your heart every morning you wake up. You try to work and earn your salvation. Like Olympic sprinter Harold Abrahams in the movie *Chariots of Fire*, we often feel like we have to justify our own existence. Just before a pivotal race, he confesses to a friend:

And now in one hour's time, I will be out there again. I will raise my eyes and look down that corridor; four feet wide, with ten lonely seconds to justify my existence. But will I?

You can imagine the anxiety he feels. You can probably relate! But the good news is that we can rest in what Christ has done instead. We no longer have to prove ourselves or justify ourselves to God or to anyone else. Because of Christ's work, we can rest. Breathe. Give thanks. It is finished.

Main Point

The instrument of justification is faith in Christ alone; it is a saving grace where the believer receives and rests upon Christ as He is offered in the gospel.

Questions for Reflection

- What does it means to be saved 'by faith' ?

- What might it look like to 'receive' Christ through faith? What might it look like to 'rest' in Christ through faith?
- In what ways, relationships, or activities do you often try to 'justify your existence' before God, others, and even yourself?

7. The Finality of Justification

════════

THE SIMPLE JOY OF A COMPLETED TASK

I like finishing things. There is a deep sense of satisfaction wrapped up in the completion of a task or project. Personally, having things in my life that I can 'finish' or complete is particularly meaningful. Since I serve as a pastor, my work is often open-ended and never finished. Sure, there are stopping places and moments when you can look back and survey progress made. However, when your work revolves around people and the ministry of the Church there is a sense in which the work is never finished. This is why I actually like mowing the lawn (most of the time). I can finish it. Even though the grass grows back (too fast), I can rest in a job well done and savor the simple joy of a completed task. Maybe you can relate?

ONCE FOR ALL

Priests and Levites in the Old Testament could relate. Similar to different types of work today, their job was never finished. Every day, week, month, and year there was ritual work to be done. The tabernacle or temple needed to be cared for and sacrifices needed to be performed. We often miss this, but their work was a back-breaking, bloody business. Every day they were killing animals to make sacrifices for not only the sins of the people, but for their own sins. This was the way it was for a long time – generation after generation.

And then something changed. Jesus arrived and fulfilled the whole sacrificial system in Himself. This is what the whole book of Hebrews is trying to make clear. In a paradoxical way, Jesus became not only the great High Priest making a sacrifice in the true temple of heaven, but also the very sacrifice as well. He was the Lamb of God who had come to take away the sins of the world (John 1:29, 36; Rev. 5:6, 12). As you can imagine, this flipped everything on its head for ancient Jews and the early Church, who were trying to make sense of what it means to faithfully follow God. It changes everything for us as well as we reflect on the doctrine of justification.

In making his case, the author of Hebrews repeats a phrase to make clear what Christ has done in His sacrificial death: 'once for all' (Heb. 7:27; 9:12, 26; 10:10). By this, the author of Hebrews indicates that Jesus' one, perfect sacrifice of His own self replaces and fulfills the repeated, daily sacrifices made by the priests for the people of God. Before, the daily sacrifices made sense. But now that Jesus has arrived and finished His work on our behalf these sacrifices can cease. The author of Hebrews connects this for us when he writes:

*For it was indeed fitting that we should have **such a high priest, holy, innocent, unstained, separated from sinners, and exalted above the heavens.** He has no need, like those high priests, to offer sacrifices daily, first for his own sins and then for those of the people, **since he did this once for all when he offered up himself.** (Heb. 7:26-27, emphasis added).*

This is really good news! Jesus is a new type of priest. He is a new type of sacrifice. Something more permanent and substantial was accomplished when Jesus went about His priestly work. The author reinforces this point as he continues along these lines in the rest of the letter:

*But when Christ appeared as a high priest of the good things that have come, then **through the greater and more perfect tent** (not made with hands, that is, not of this creation) he entered **once for all** into the holy places, not by means of the blood of goats and calves but by means of **his own blood**, thus **securing an eternal redemption** ... But as it is, he has appeared **once for all** at the end of the ages to put away sin by the sacrifice of himself. (Heb. 9:11-12, 26b, emphasis added)*

This is what theologians are referring to when they talk about the 'finished work' of Christ. This is why Jesus said 'it is finished' when He died on the Cross (John 19:30). Justification is final because Jesus has finished His work – 'once for all.' It's done! Our justification is final and secured by Him. And it's all of grace! That's why the Westminster Shorter Catechism says that justification is 'an *act* of God's free grace.'[1] It is something that God through Christ

---

1   Westminster Shorter Catechism, Q&A #33.

has accomplished on our behalf and graciously applies to us by His Holy Spirit. The work is done and we can rest in Christ. There is a wonderful finality to our justification.

JUSTIFICATION'S JOURNEY

And yet, we can add another beautiful dimension to this truth. Like a caterpillar's journey to becoming a butterfly, our justification developed and came to fruition in stages. Our justification was determined in eternity, accomplished in history, and experienced definitively in our own lives.[2]

God decreed that His people would be justified before creation (Gal. 3:8, 1 Pet. 1:2, 19-20; Rom. 8:30), Christ died and rose for our justification in the fullness of time (Gal. 4:4; 1 Tim. 2:6; Rom. 4:25), and we are definitively justified when we place our faith in Christ (Col. 1:21-22; Gal. 2:16; Titus 3:4-7). This adds even more weight to the significance of the finality of our justification. God has been at work in it from eternity past. Christ, with great love and intention, won it through His sweat and tears. By the Spirit's power, God has faithfully brought it to fruition in our lives.

---

2   Van Dixhoorn, Chad, *Confessing the Faith*, 167-70.

SO WHAT?

The finality of justification provides us with a firm foundation to rest on as we go about our lives as Christians. Instead of anxiously worrying about if we have done enough or measure up, we can rest assured that nothing more is needed from us in order to hear God say, 'well done, good and faithful servant... enter into the joy of your Master' (Matt. 25:23) on the day we die or when Christ returns. That fact is already settled because we are justified in Christ – once for all.

This changes our relationship with God fundamentally. We are unshakably God's adopted children now. Instead of living out of fear and uncertainty, our lives become the overflow of gratitude and thankfulness. As 'living sacrifices' (Rom. 12:1) we offer ourselves freely to God in everything just as Christ offered Himself freely for us and on our behalf. The finality of justification unlocks our love: our love for God and for one another. The hymnwriter William Cowper captures this effect of God's justifying love on us when he writes:

Then all my servile works were done,
A righteousness to raise

Now, freely chosen in the Son,
I freely choose His ways.[3]

There is more to say about this in terms of how justification connects to our growing in personal holiness (sanctification), but for now it is important to highlight the permanence of our justification. The finality of justification is a source of encouragement and comfort for all believers. It is finished – thanks be to God!

Main Point

Our justification is final because of the finished work of Jesus.

Questions for Reflection

- What simple tasks do you find joy in completing? Why is finishing something enjoyable?
- How do you think the Old Testament priests felt having to carry out the same bloody sacrifices every day? What do you think God was trying to communicate to the people through the sacrificial system of the Old Testament?

---

3   Cowper, William, 'Love Constraining to Obedience.'

- How is Jesus a new kind of priest? How might resting in His finished work have daily, practical effects on the way we go about our lives?

8. The Benefits of Justification

━━━━━━

We love books in my family. As a pastor I have many books and collect them for all sorts of purposes. But even more so, we love children's books – we have loads of them. My kids may have more than me! One of our favorites by Sally Lloyd-Jones tells the story of Little Red Squirrel and his daddy. As they go about their day exploring and playing, Little Red Squirrel peppers his father with questions trying to guess the reason that his daddy loves him. Is it because he is a good climber, brave, fast, handsome, friendly, or good at finding hidden berries? Though never guessing the correct answer, his daddy responds playfully and affectionately. As his daddy tucks him into bed after a full and fun day, he leans in close and finally reveals the answer:

Little Red Squirrel, you are very fast, and smart, and handsome, and friendly, and good at finding berries...and you are very strong and brave... But that's not why I love you...No, little one...I love you just because you're mine.[1]

This beautiful and sweet book is a wonderful picture for us of some of the rich benefits we have in our justification. We belong to God and we have His love in full – not because we have done anything, but because we are His and He is ours. In justification, we have God as our Abba Father. And with that new relationship comes peace, grace, joy, and hope. There is much to treasure here!

THE BENEFITS OF JUSTIFICATION

The Apostle Paul unpacks some of this for us in the book of Romans. In fact, chapters 3-6 are dedicated to exploring the doctrine of justification and its implications for the Christian life. At the beginning of chapter 5, Paul summarizes some of the benefits we receive in justification:

Therefore, since we have been justified by faith, we have peace with God through our Lord Jesus Christ. Through him we have also

---

1   Lloyd-Jones, Sally, *Just Because You're Mine* (New York: HarperCollins, 2012).

obtained access by faith into this grace in which we stand, and we rejoice in hope of the glory of God. Not only that, but we rejoice in our sufferings, knowing that suffering produces endurance, and endurance produces character, and character produces hope, and hope does not put us to shame, because God's love has been poured into our hearts through the Holy Spirit who has been given to us. (Rom. 5:1-5)

Paul starts off by saying 'since we have been justified by faith' to indicate that what follows is a result or benefit of our justification. First of all, he says, we 'have peace with God through our Lord Jesus Christ.' Before we were alienated from God and even His enemies in our sinful rebellion against Him. Like the end of a great war, hostilities have ceased. But even more so, we are reconciled with God – not simply His conquered subjects, not just His servants, but His adopted children, enjoying the wholeness of intimacy with Him. How did this come to be? It is only through the person and work of our Lord Jesus Christ.

Going further, Paul indicates that we 'have also obtained access by faith into this grace in which we stand.' By faith and in our justification, we now have access to God. We have direct access to the throne room of the Heavenly King, who is also our loving Father. This means we can pray to Him – out loud, in our thoughts, on our own, or with a room full of people – and know that He hears, and He cares. The author of Hebrews captures this reality when he writes, 'Let us then with confidence draw near to the throne of grace, that we may receive mercy and find grace to help in time of need' (Heb. 4:16). With confidence, we can draw near to God and receive the fullness of His grace. This is true at all times, but, most encouragingly, at our times of greatest need. We can have confidence because of this and have a firm foundation with God on which 'we stand.'

Paul continues by listing a third benefit: 'we rejoice in hope of the glory of God.' This makes sense. The peace and intimacy we have with God through justification leads to joy – not just joy of what God has accomplished but also of what He further intends to do for His people. When we sing in church, that's just one way in which we encourage each other to celebrate God's goodness to us. We can have enduring joy that flows out of our hope in God's promise to glorify us with Christ on the last day as fellow recipients of resurrection (Rom. 8:29-30; John 17:24; 1 Cor. 15:42-55). Hope is future-oriented faith.[2] Because of what Christ has done for us and now dwelling in Him, we have 'strength for today and bright hope for tomorrow.'[3] By meditating on this future reality we begin to rejoice in hope.

JOY IN SUFFERING

The Christian hope is a sturdy hope. Paul goes on to indicate that this joy in Christ persists and is even able to be expressed 'in our sufferings.' Life is hard sometimes, and we're not guaranteed an easy ride. All other joys may be taken away but this joy is found in the *hope* of the fulfillment of what God has promised. This is remarkable and other-worldly! Naturally, we look at our sufferings – grief, loss, pain, disappointment, uncertainty, and more – as the thieves of our joy. But in our new justified status, Paul is saying that our sufferings become the very source of our rejoicing.

How does that work? Well, we are not to rejoice in our sufferings in and of themselves

---

2   See Mark Jones, *Faith, Hope and Love: The Christ-Centered Way to Grow in Grace* (Wheaton, IL: Crossway, 2017), pp.100-104.

3   Chisholm, Thomas O., 'Great Is Thy Faithfulness.'

– they are the result of sin, the effects of the Fall, and evil at work in the world. Rather, as justified people, we are enabled to rejoice in our sufferings because of what they bring and where they lead. There is an unbreakable chain here. Paul says that 'suffering produces endurance, endurance produces character, and character produces hope' (Rom. 5:3-4). Like an athlete in training experiences the pain of the necessary exercises to develop in their craft, Christians grow stronger and firmer in their hope in the glory of God through suffering. And this hope is sure! How? 'Because God's love has been poured into our hearts through the Holy Spirit who has been given to us.' God's enduring love for us through our suffering gives us good reason to continue in hope and joy.

ASSURANCE AND CONFIDENCE

The last thing that Paul says here touches on something else that is a benefit of justification. He talks about the Holy Spirit who is given to believers and is the means by which God's love is poured into their hearts. When we place our faith in Christ, the Holy Spirit comes to dwell within us and works to assure us of God's love for us. This is what theologians call the 'assurance of salvation.' There is an element of this assurance embedded in the very nature of our faith in Christ. If you trust in Christ alone for salvation, you can be assured that God loves you with a 'Never-Stopping, Never Giving Up, Unbreaking, Always and Forever Love.'[4] This ought to fill us with a deep joy and confidence and spills over into every aspect of our lives. Sinclair Ferguson summarizes this well when he writes,

The [one] who knows [they are] justified is a [person] of unbounded confidence and assurance. [They] knows that none of [their] failures can ever change the divine verdict. It is guaranteed and settled forever in heaven.[5]

Out of this sure and settled place of love and justification, we are empowered to live holy lives where we can rejoice even in the midst of sorrow and suffering. Even in our greatest losses, most colossal failures, and deepest griefs we can be assured that we belong to God in love. He is at work, and will deliver us again (2 Cor. 1:8-10). Even on our darkest day, we can have confidence underneath the sorrow

---

4   Lloyd-Jones, Sally, *The Jesus Storybook Bible* (Grand Rapids, MI: Zondervan, 2012).

5   Ferguson, Sinclair B., *The Christian Life*, 91.

that perseveres because of the work of the Holy Spirit within us. Out of this we are empowered to do good works as an overflow of gratitude and in hopeful expectation of what is to come. In justification, we have many wonderful benefits!

Main Point

The rich benefits of justification include peace with God, access to His grace, joy even in suffering, a sure hope in Christ, and the power and motivation to do good works.

Questions for Reflection

- Why does God love you? How do you know this? How can someone find assurance of God's love for them?
- How is being someone's beloved child different than being their servant? How do we make the change from servant to child in our relationship with God? What does it look like to live as a beloved child of God?
- What different approach does Christianity take toward suffering? What does it look like to 'rejoice in your sufferings' without denying or suppressing the pain and difficulty of them?

9. Justification and Sanctification[1]

DON'T BE BOBBY NEWPORT

In the fourth season of the popular TV comedy *Parks and Recreation*, main character Leslie Knope finally has the opportunity to pursue her lifelong dream of running for a City Council seat in her hometown of Pawnee, Indiana. While highly qualified, Leslie finds herself behind in the polls to a ridiculous but popular opponent: Bobby Newport. Bobby is the heir to Sweetums family business that employs a large portion of the town. He has a great fortune and has used it to live a lavishly irresponsible life of idiocy and immaturity into his forties. Though Bobby

---

1 For more on this topic, read *A Student's Guide to Sanctification* by Ligon Duncan and John Perritt (Fearn: Christian Focus Publications, 2020).

can be innocently charming, he has become wildly entitled.

When the race turns in Leslie's favor, he begs Leslie to quit her campaign. Incredulous, she asks why she would do that. Bobby responds, 'Because, I want it. Come on, give it to me. Gimme it, gimme it, come on gimme it. Give me the election! I'm sorry, please... Please.' While awkwardly funny for the audience, this moment is embarrassing and humiliating for Bobby. Instead of becoming mature, generous, and hard-working, Bobby had allowed his great riches to shape him for the worst. When it mattered, it showed.

In a similar way, in the gospel we have been given great riches! In justification, we have been forgiven and gifted the righteousness of Christ. We have been adopted into the very family of God. We are considered holy in God's sight and will be glorified with Christ at His return. We are indwelled by the Holy Spirit and kept by Him until then. Even so, it is possible for us to be like Bobby Newport – to squander our riches by living immaturely and selfishly. We too can become entitled.

CONTINUING IN SIN?

The Apostle Paul anticipates this potential problem in the book of Romans. In light of the grace we've been shown, he asks an important question: 'What shall we say then? Are we to continue in sin that grace may abound?' (Rom. 6:1). In this, Paul is picking up on a common response to God's free grace. One could think: *if God will graciously forgive when I sin, then it doesn't matter if I keep on sinning – because He will always love me and forgive me anyway.* There is a logic to this. However, it's not gospel logic. Paul wants to make this clear when he responds emphatically:

> *By no means! How can we who died to sin still live in it? Do you not know that all of us who have been baptized into Christ Jesus were baptized into his death? We were buried therefore with him by baptism into death, in order that, just as Christ was raised from the dead by the glory of the Father, we too might walk in newness of life. (Rom. 6:2-4)*

Paul wants us to see the big picture. Christ died for us to free us from sin! Christ rose from the dead that we 'might walk in newness of life' like Him – in obedience and maturity. It is wrongheaded, therefore, to flippantly continue in patterns of sin. Our justification is inseparably connected to our sanctification. Because we are justified, we are to make progress in holiness – in the process of sanctification. While it is true that we are reckoned perfectly righteous in God's sight in justification, He intends for us to more and more become who we have been made to be in Christ in the process of sanctification – in the day-to-day of our lives.

LIGHT AND HEAT

In making sense of this, it is important to understand that while justification and sanctification are distinct, they are inseparable. This is of vital importance in the Christian life and has been a major point of emphasis in the history of the Church. Reformer John Calvin labored to make this clear in his ministry and gives us a helpful analogy for understanding the relationship between justification and sanctification. He explained that the two doctrines are like the light and heat of the sun – they always accompany each other though they are different parts of the sun's energy.[2] The light of the sun shines on us as we simultaneously feel its heat. They're different, but you can't separate them. In the same way, sanctification always accompanies justification and is dependent upon it. Separating these two teachings, Calvin warns us, would be to tear apart the gospel and even 'divide Christ himself.'

So, justification and sanctification are different, but always go together. But this is the distinction: we receive Christ's righteousness by faith in justification and we grow in righteousness by faith in process of daily repentance (turning from sin and idols and toward God) in sanctification. Justification is an '*act* of God's free grace,'[3] while sanctification is a '*work* of God's free grace,'[4] where we participate with God in the renewal of His image in us. Even so, these two always accompany one another like the light and heat of the sun's rays. We get into big trouble when we miss or forget this – we even divide Christ in a sense!

---

2   Calvin, John. *Tracts and Letters*, Vol. III, 115-16.

3   Westminster Shorter Catechism, Q&A #33.

4   Ibid., Q&A #35.

FAITH AND WORKS

And yet, justification provides the power and motivation in our sanctification. Because we are God's justified children, we now go and live as His children empowered by His Spirit and motivated by the love of God poured out for us in Christ. The Apostle Paul demonstrates this dynamic in Ephesians 2:4-10. We are saved by grace through faith on the basis of Christ's righteousness – not our own works. We are justified in Him. Because of this, we are His 'workmanship.' And yet, as Christ's new creations, we were re-created 'in Christ Jesus for good works, which God prepared beforehand, that we should walk in them.' Our doing of good works, our growth in holiness and Christian maturity, our sanctification flows out of our justification. We have been made new and now we are to live as those new people. This new status and life manifests itself in a life of faithful, loving obedience.

In fact, if our faith in Christ does not bear this type of fruit we may be in trouble. James looks at this dynamic from the other side: 'So also faith by itself, if it does not have works, is dead' (James 2:17). Yes, we are justified by faith in Christ alone, but that faith does not remain alone. James rightly sees the problem with this. Paul and James are in harmony with one another. Good works and progress in practical holiness naturally ought to follow faith in Christ. In a sense, good works prove the existence of true faith, like smoke reveals the existence of a flame. Sanctification is inseparable from justification and naturally flows out of it.

FREED FROM, FREED TO

Another helpful way to think of this gospel dynamic is in terms of freedom. In justification we are *freed from* both the curse of the law and from any burden to keep the law's demands to enter into God's favor.[5] But we are also *freed to* 'delight in and obey [God's] law that we once hated and rejected (Rom. 8:7-8).'[6] This is the basis for our progress in sanctification. God's words and commands become sweeter than honey to us (Ps. 19:10; 119:103). Our desires are progressively reshaped by the Holy Spirit to want to obey His commands. In this, we find true freedom: to walk with God in His paths – glorifying and enjoying Him forever – as an expression of thankfulness and gratitude for the

---

5   Waters, Guy. *A Christian's Pocket Guide to Being Made Right with God*, 33.

6   Ibid., 36.

free gospel of grace.[7] Unlike Bobby Newport, our gospel riches ought to lead us to gratitude and a life of joyful, thankful obedience and responsibility as God's beloved children.

Main Point

Justification serves as the foundation and motive for the process of sanctification.

Questions for Reflection

- How can entitlement become a big problem in relationships? How can it cause problems spiritually in our relationship with God?
- How is sinning in response to receiving God's grace not an expression of 'gospel logic' ? In what ways does Jesus intend to reorient and reshape us as His followers?
- How are justification and sanctification connected in the Christian life? How do they differ?
- How are faith and works supposed to be related to each other in the Christian life? Why is lovingly obeying God and selflessly serving others the path of true freedom?

---

7   Westminster Shorter Catechism, Q&A #1.

Conclusion: The Gospel is Rest

The doctrine of justification is fundamental to the Christian faith. But I hope that through this book you have been able to reflect on how practical it is as well. A right and clear understanding of justification is essential for Christian joy to flourish and for God's love to be multiplied in one's life. In a world and culture that highly touts what you can do and how much you can earn – a society of constant proving and one-upmanship – embracing and applying justification is the pathway to rest in God and a life of flourishing.

THE GOSPEL IS REST

A friend of mine named Cameron Cole learned this over several years in his life. Though he grew up in the church, Cameron found that he had completely misunderstood (or had not appropriated) the concept of God's grace in justification. However, this did not come to the forefront for him until he was in high school and college. Describing his belief system up to that point, Cameron writes,

> ...*[it] revolved around accepting Jesus for salvation, sharing Christ with others, and then trying really, really hard for God out of my own strength, using Jesus as my role model...my personal theology translated into performance – an exhausting treadmill.*[1]

Academically, athletically, and socially, Cameron overloaded his calendar and amassed accolades. He finished college a year early as a double major and earned a master's degree during his fourth year, all while also starting a non-profit organization. As this pace continued after college, Cameron began to experience the effects on his mental health: he began having problems with his short-term memory, would easily lose his train of thought, and had difficulty sleeping, while wrestling with oppressive fear and anxiety surrounding his work.

---

1   Cole, Cameron. 'The Gospel at the Heart of All Things' in *Gospel Centered Youth-Ministry* (Wheaton, IL: Crossway, 2016), 34.

In a pivotal moment, Cameron met with his pastor to receive some help and insight. His pastor insisted that it seemed like Cameron was heading towards a nervous breakdown and needed to take some practical steps for his health's sake, but he also drew Cameron's attention to his lack of understanding of the gospel of grace. Cameron says his life was forever changed when his pastor said,

The gospel is rest. The gospel means Jesus carries the burden of your life. The gospel means you will never have to prove yourself again, because Jesus has proven you on the cross.[2]

Though Cameron had not yet hit his 'rock bottom,' his pastor's gentle and wise counsel would transform the way he saw God, himself, and his life. Fundamentally, the gospel means that we can rest from proving ourselves because Christ has proven us in His finished work. Out of this rest, we can rejoice and truly live.

ARE YOU RESTING?

By making it this far, you will have thought much about justification and its implications for

---

2   Ibid., 35.

your life. My friend, have you taken it to heart? Have you received Christ's forgiveness and righteousness as freely offered in the gospel of grace? Are you resting in Christ? It is only when we, like Cameron, start here that we can truly live the life of a justified person into which our Heavenly Father has called us. Justification is a glorious truth! It ought not ever get boring or become inconsequential to us. In it we are drawn close to God in Christ and are freed to truly live with Him – now and into eternity. By grace and through faith in the finished work of Christ, we are made right with God and can rest from our self-justifying labors. Drink that in. Breathe in with satisfaction the restful peace that Christ has won for you. And as you breathe out, may you be able to pray with the hymnwriter:

Jesus, I am resting, resting,
In the joy of what thou art;
I am finding out the greatness
Of thy loving heart.[3]

---

3   Pigott, Jean Sophia. 'Jesus, I Am Resting, Resting.'

Appendix A: What Now?

- Stop and analyze your own heart. Do you truly believe in Jesus Christ? Have you repented of your sin and placed your faith in His finished work?
- Thank God for being so gracious and faithful as to make you His child!
- Reflect upon the wickedness of your sin and what Jesus did to pay for it.
- Reflect upon the reality that you are truly righteous because of what Jesus did.
- Are you living under constant guilt? Is it because you're trying to earn your own righteousness before God?
- Is the truth of justification central to your life? Are you resting in the finished work of Christ? How can you tell?
- Step back a little bit and consider how your life story fits into God's big Story. How does the big Story make sense of your story?

How does your story fit into the big Story? How is your story a continuation of the big Story?

- Think about your daily rhythms and habits. How could you deepen your understanding of your justification and its implications? In what ways do you need to change as a result of God's love for you in Christ? How can you better remind yourself of the truth of justification on a daily basis?

- Consider how being justified in Christ might free and empower you to serve God and others. How and where is God freeing and empowering you to serve in your life right now?

- Think about your relationships and the people that are a part of your life right now. With whom could you share the good news of Christ? How can you gently and respectfully share your joy and hope in Christ with them?

Appendix B: Other Resources on this Topic

STARTING OUT

Brian Cosby, *Rebels Rescued: A Student's Guide to Reformed Theology* (Fearn: Christian Focus Publications, 2018)

J.V. Fesko, *What Is Justification by Faith Alone?* (Phillipsburg, NJ: P&R, 2012)

Greg Gilbert, *What Is the Gospel?* (Wheaton, IL: Crossway, 2010)

J.I. Packer, *Concise Theology: A Guide to Historic Christian Beliefs* (Downers Grove, IL: IVP, 1993)

Guy Waters, *A Christian's Pocket Guide to Being Made Right with God* (Fearn: Christian Focus Publications, 2012)

The Westminster Confession of Faith and Catechisms

DIGGING DEEPER

Jerry Bridges, *The Gospel for Real Life: Turning to the Liberating Power of the Cross...Every Day* (Colorado Springs, CO: NavPress, 2003)

Sinclair B. Ferguson, *The Christian Life: A Doctrinal Introduction* (Edinburgh: Banner of Truth, 1981)

Timothy J. Keller, *The Prodigal God: Recovering the Heart of the Christian Faith* (New York: Penguin, 2008)

John Piper, *Counted Righteous in Christ: Should We Abandon the Imputation of Christ's Righteousness?* (Wheaton, IL: Crossway, 2002)

O. Palmer Robertson, *The Christ of the Covenants* (Phillipsburg, NJ: P&R, 1981)

R.C. Sproul, *Faith Alone: The Evangelical Doctrine of Justification* (Ada, MI: Baker Books, 1995)

MORE PLEASE!

J.V. Fesko, *Justification: Understanding the Classic Reformed Doctrine* (Phillipsburg, NJ: P&R, 2012)

Richard B. Gaffin, *By Faith, Not by Sight: Paul and the Order of Salvation* (Phillipsburg, NJ: P&R, 2013)

John Murray, *Redemption Accomplished and Applied* (Grand Rapids, MI: Eerdmans, 2015)

John Piper, *The Future of Justification: A Response to N.T. Wright* (Downers Grove, IL: IVP, 1993)

Glossary

Adoption – An act of God's grace where He makes believers in Christ His children, where they enjoy all the blessings and benefits of being such. It is founded on justification and the blessing of the justified. It consists of a new relational status with God as members of His family.

Assurance – One of the many spiritual benefits that flow from justification, sanctification, and adoption, where believers enjoy a certainty of belonging to God as a redeemed child of God. It is founded upon the promises of God, the inward evidence of God at work within us, and the testimony of the Holy Spirit that witnesses to our belonging to Him. It accompanies saving faith but can, for various reasons, be weakened in the experience of believers.

Covenant – A covenant is an expression of God 'coming down to our level' to help us in our state as needy sinners, by binding Himself to us in love through the making of promises. It is a relationship of love that leads to a contract being made between the two parties. Life-and-death promises (or vows) are made from one to the other. Blessings and curses are associated with keeping and breaking these agreements.

Covenant of Creation (or Covenant of Works) – The first covenant that God made with mankind in the Garden of Eden, where He promised life to Adam (and his descendants) upon the condition of perfect and personal obedience to His command not to eat of the tree of the knowledge of good and evil. Adam (and Eve) violated this covenant and no one else can keep it due to mankind's inherited sin nature.

Covenant of Grace – The second covenant that God made with mankind after Adam and Eve violated the Covenant of Creation. It is the gracious agreement between the offended God and the offending but elect sinner, in which God promises salvation through faith in Christ, and the sinner accepts this believingly, promising a life of faith and obedience. It has 'two administrations' – that of the Old Testament (First Gospel, Noah, Abraham, Moses, David) and the New Testament (New Covenant through Christ).

Doctrine – A teaching or collection of teachings on a particular subject.

Faith – Belief and trust in Jesus Christ as He is offered in the gospel. It is a gift of God's grace and the channel by which we receive and rest in the forgiveness of sins, Christ's righteousness, and all other spiritual blessings promised in the Christian life.

God the Father – God is one Being and three Persons; referred to as the Trinity. The Father, the Son, and the Holy Spirit make up the three Persons of the One God. Each Person is eternal and equal in essence. God the Father is the Creator of all things and rules over everything. God, in His grace, promised to save His sinful children from their rebellion. He adopts His children through the finished work of His Son, Jesus.

Good Works – The spiritual and logical expression of saving faith, where believers work out their salvation through deeds of love and mercy in accordance with God's law of love. They grow out of faith, while at the same time bearing witness to the existence and vitality of that faith.

Grace – The undeserved favor and goodness of God poured out on His enemies. When God makes you His child, it is because of His grace alone. Grace is not something you can earn.

Holy/Holiness – Set apart, different. God is infinitely and eternally 'other' and completely set apart from all beings. When Christians strive by grace to live holy lives, they will be set apart and different from the world.

Holy Spirit – God is one Being and three Persons; referred to as the Trinity. The Father, the Son, and the Holy Spirit make up the three Persons of the One God. Each Person is eternal and equal in essence. The Holy Spirit is often referred to as the strength of the Christian. The Spirit is given to all believers and helps us live every aspect of the Christian life.

Imputed – Something that is ascribed to another vicariously. This is often used as an adjective for righteousness or guilt, where Christ's righteousness is ascribed to believers and the sins of believers are ascribed to Christ by faith.

In Christ – A Christian is completely united to Christ. The phrase 'in Christ' is repeated throughout the Bible and this refers to our union with Him. We are completely secure as God's children and no one can take that away.

Jesus Christ – God is one Being and three Persons; referred to as the Trinity. The Father, the Son, and the Holy Spirit make up the three Persons of the One God. Each Person is eternal and equal in essence. Jesus Christ is God's eternal Son. Jesus Christ is fully God and has always been in existence. He appears at times in the Old Testament, but He added flesh to His deity when He was born of a virgin birth by the Holy Spirit. He lived a perfect life and died a death on the Cross for God's children. He is the only Savior of sinners.

Justification – The one-time act where God declared His children righteous, by the finished work of His Son Jesus. Jesus lived a fully righteous life and gives that righteousness to His Father's children, by faith. Jesus also took the sins of God's children on Himself when He died on the Cross. That one-time act – 'It is finished' – justified God's children.

Law – In a general sense, this refers to God's perfect design and way of life for His creation. Since sin has entered the world, God's people cannot perfectly keep His law and are therefore declared guilty. Since God is a perfectly just judge and His law reveals His good character, He sent Jesus to perfectly obey the law for His children.

Redemption – God's work of perfecting His sinful children through the work of the Spirit and Jesus.

Regeneration – Spiritual rebirth, where God renovates the heart and implants a new dynamic within a person that shows itself through a positive and receptive response to the gospel and to Jesus Himself. It is entirely an act of God's grace by the power of the Holy Spirit.

Repentance – An act of God's grace that moves sinners to turn from their sin and turn to Jesus. In order to be a Christian, we must repent of our sin and place our faith in Jesus. That said, repentance is a continual practice of Christians since we battle with sin until we go to heaven.

Sanctification – This is the essence of the Christian life. This is the ongoing work of Christians fighting against sin and living in a righteous/holy/godly way. Christians cannot work in their own strength; they can only work by the power of the Holy Spirit.

Sin – It is anti-God; sin is completely opposed to all that is good and is so horrible, it took the death of God's Son to save us. It is thinking, saying, or doing anything that God forbids in the Bible. It can also refer to disobeying God's commands. Sin brings every form of pain, suffering, and sadness into God's creation.

Sovereignty – God's complete rule and reign over all creation. Kings can also be referred to as Sovereigns, so this term points to God's Kingly rule over everyone and everything.

Theology – The study of God; vital to the life of a Christian. To love Jesus well, Christians must strive to have a solid theology from the Bible.

Word (of God) – The Bible or Scriptures. Since God wrote the entire Bible through humans, we call it God's Word.

Works (Righteousness) – refers to a practice where people try to earn God's favor. When people believe they can work their way to heaven by their own 'good' works. This goes against the teaching of the Bible. Jesus was the only righteous one and He gives us His righteous works by faith.

Reformed Youth Ministries (RYM) exists to reach students for Christ and equip them to serve. Passing the faith on to the next generation has been RYM's passion since it began. In 1972 three youth workers who shared a passion for biblical teaching to youth surveyed the landscape of youth ministry conferences. What they found was an emphasis on fun and games, not God's Word. Therefore, they started a conference that focused on the preaching and teaching of God's Word. Over the years RYM has grown beyond conferences into three areas of ministry: conferences, training, and resources.

- **Conferences:** RYM's youth conferences take place in the summer at a variety of locations across the United States and are continuing to expand. We also host parenting conferences throughout the year at local churches.

- **Training:** RYM launched an annual Youth Leader Training (YLT) conference in 2008. YLT has grown steadily through the years and is offered in multiple locations. RYM also offers a Church Internship Program in partnering local churches as well as youth leader coaching and youth ministry consulting.
- **Resources:** RYM offers a variety of resources for leaders, parents, and students. Several Bible studies are offered as free downloads with more titles regularly being added to their catalogue. RYM hosts multiple podcasts: *Parenting Today*, *The Local Youth Worker*, and *The RYM Student Podcast*, all of which can be downloaded on multiple formats. There are many additional ministry tools available for download on the website.

If you are passionate for passing the faith on to the next generation, please visit www.rym.org to learn more about Reformed Youth Ministries. If you are interested in partnering with us in ministry, please visit www.rym.org/donate.

Watch out for other forthcoming books in the
Track series, including:

JOE
DEEGAN
SERIES EDITED BY
JOHN PERRITT

A Student's Guide to the Power of Story

JOE DEEGAN

Stories are powerful. They shape us and stay with us in a way that nothing else does. Ideas and wisdom can be portrayed in a way that draws the listener or reader in. Stories can build relationships and understanding. They can help to make sense of confusing concepts. In this compelling addition to the *Track* series, Joe Deegan explains why stories are so important – and what role they play in our everyday lives.

978-1-5271-0695-6

WALT MUELLER
SERIES EDITED BY
JOHN PERRITT

A Student's Guide to Navigating Culture

WALT MUELLER

We all belong to a culture. From the shows we watch to the language we use to the food we eat; culture shapes the way we look at the world, the way we act, the way we think. It affects so much of our lives, and yet we are rarely aware of it. If we are not careful, it can push us away from God's good desires for who we are and how we live in our world.

978-1-5271-0694-9

A Student's Guide to Glorification

Derek W. H. Thomas

In this short book for young adults, Derek Thomas explains what the Bible means when it talks about glory. Beginning with the Creation, he explains how the reflection of God's glory was not completely destroyed when sin entered the world, but it was broken. Thomas then goes on to explain how this glory of God was perfectly represented in the person of Jesus; how it is partially restored in Christians; and how it will be perfectly restored in the new heavens and the new earth.

978-1-5271-0694-9

Christian Focus Publications

Our mission statement —

STAYING FAITHFUL

In dependence upon God we seek to impact the world through literature faithful to His infallible Word, the Bible. Our aim is to ensure that the Lord Jesus Christ is presented as the only hope to obtain forgiveness of sin, live a useful life and look forward to heaven with Him.

Our books are published in four imprints:

CHRISTIAN
FOCUS

Popular works including biographies, commentaries, basic doctrine and Christian living.

CHRISTIAN
HERITAGE

Books representing some of the best material from the rich heritage of the church.

MENTOR

Books written at a level suitable for Bible College and seminary students, pastors, and other serious readers. The imprint includes commentaries, doctrinal studies, examination of current issues and church history.

CF4•K

Children's books for quality Bible teaching and for all age groups: Sunday school curriculum, puzzle and activity books; personal and family devotional titles, biographies and inspirational stories — because you are never too young to know Jesus!

Christian Focus Publications Ltd,
Geanies House, Fearn, Ross-shire,
IV20 1TW, Scotland, United Kingdom.
www.christianfocus.com
blog.christianfocus.com